Selwyn Pritchard

STIRRING STUFF

SINCLAIR-STEVENSON

First published in Great Britain 1993
by Sinclair-Stevenson
an imprint of Reed Consumer Books Ltd
Michelin House, 81 Fulham Road, London SW3 6RB
and Auckland, Melbourne, Singapore and Toronto

Copyright © 1993 by Selwyn Pritchard
ISBN 1-85619-308-X

A CIP catalogue record for this book
is available at the British Library

Typeset by Rowland Phototypesetting Ltd
Bury St Edmunds, Suffolk
Printed in Great Britain by
Clays Ltd, St Ives plc

for
Margaret and Stanley Middleton

Acknowledgements

Some of these poems were previously published in
Being Determined (1990), by The Cornford Press,
Launceston, Tasmania, Australia. Most have appeared
in magazines and newspapers in the United Kingdom and
Eire, Canada and the USA, Australia and New Zealand,
notably in *Critical Survey, Encounter*, the *Guardian, Honest
Ulsterman, New Welsh Review, Planet, Poetry Wales* (UK);
Poetry Ireland, Krino (Eire); *Age Monthly Review, Overland,
Southerly, Sydney Morning Herald, Westerly* (Australia); *Ariel,
Poetry Canada, Wascana Review* (Canada); *Iowa Review,
Maryland Poetry Review, South Dakota Review* (USA).

Contents

The Shaky Islands

Apple Isle

Island Continent

Peninsula

THE
SHAKY
ISLANDS

Calls of Nature

Before dawn is the time
for middle-aged poems.
Then the paunched man clenches an eye
on stars' slow-pulsing, cold regard:

solitary representative
but competent to reflect
equal mystery before turning
covers of dreams or earth and
melting into their
warmth.

Day's Bay, Wellington

Wartime

warmed coins melt spy holes
in frost fronds the red sun flames
school milk thaws on pipes

pencil shavings smell
sharp as harvest straws chalk wax
crayon 'Number One'

dad's waistcoat yields pinched
fags pencil stubs his dad's watch
HUSH! Six-o-clock News

old soldier he hefts
my brother's kitbag through snow
to the train mum cries

by frames memory unwinds from fifty years
railway tracks and buttons bright as tears

Day's Bay, Wellington

The Tempest: Rain Stopped Play

The first scene with sailors was a disaster.
Then Prospero strode the grass,
spark-eyed and wry-cheeked, irked,
being short, by his magic cloak's hem,
he did not see Fluff (or Clio?) pad through.

Laughter made him fly at the wrong speech:
Miranda awoke with a jerk; Caliban,
that stinking fish, entered right
as all looked left.
                       At that moment the heavens split.
'Cut!' the producer yelled. Spots silvered;
tin sheets flexed as we ran for cover.

'Thank God', I gasped on the bus,
'it was not "The Winter's Tale"', but
our driver, shooting the lights,
blew a retrospective verdict on a bikie,
moths flew like snow in our beams,
down roads empty at night just now,
what with one thing and another.

Palmerston North

Switching Off

A silent tableau on the verandah,
sepia by now in regimental album,
then spurs, red jackets, gold piping and pink gin,
carols over seas of static, the sun
stooping over the hot plain's rim with none
of our British twilight. Stars, lights, fire flies
switching on: decorations: Christmas begun.
Bowtied, cigared and drunk on life, I posed.

At fifty I groan still to remember
how, temporary gentleman, I stood
and chunnered through their shibboleths and codes
until one said, 'Oh do shut up!' (Not a bad
chap, they said, plebeian of speech but could,
with effort, talk, walk, act like an officer.)
Cambridge choired Christ; chill keening. I understood
that public school ghost amongst His colonial troops.

I learned to command, charge, snub, dissemble
from Old Etonians and suave Wykehamists
Dad had obeyed, crawling over clay comrades,
amazed to survive their orders, be missed
by death; shell-shocked-loyal to the flag; pissed
on deference every Remembrance Day;
Council Yard 'Right Marker', shoving a fist
in the Union man's face: dear dead daft Dad!

Did he stand keen in the ranks in Guyana?
(The elected Blacks turned out too Red
until one dawn we called for a recount.)
Finger on trigger at the Berlin Wall said:

'Ours is not to reason why, Sir. Better dead
than slave in mind-forged manacles!' At Ground
Zero cheered President Lemming who led
world taste in candy, missiles, and old films.

I could never excuse my sad, sour shame
at his fond pride, nor the need to conceal
family and school. 'A chip-on-the-shoulder'?
Pomeranian crap! What we feel
for our kids is our essence. What ideal
could need its sacrifice? Only the interests
of the powerful to whom such truths reveal
Red heresy: evil, alarming, clearly mad!

And in that charmed group from thirty years
A General; telly star, tycoon: no surprise,
a bland and desiccated Thatcherite
strutting the steps of Number Ten, hard eyes
set on a shop-keepers' nation suffice
for crabbed elite and hard-nosed pigs to prosper,
the holy Hidden Hand (a fist) his device
to let men like Dad enjoy 'Free Enterprise.'

All night the morepork muttered, Tasman hushed.
On a summer morning over static
come fascist carols from that stone cold town
where breeding and logic are emphatic:
noblesse oblige to gild the Socratic lie:
no votes for the shiftless! Welfare
thus, like envy, is undemocratic.

I flick the switch. My sons sleep undisturbed.

Wanganui

Haiku for a Sleeping Wife

Ah, your hair which caught
my breath is grey; my strength just
this whisper at dawn.

Generations locked
us together; when loving
was lissom, flesh ached.

A daughter! Three sons!
Pearls made perfect in your lips'
fluted secrecy.

You sewed, I read, snow
fell and fled; children slept, grew.
This we thought we planned.

In your bones I feel
our certainty, but warm,
smile against the dark.

Eastbourne

New Zeal

birds' simplicities shaped
                                    raw land
streamed shook up shrill vortices
settling in bones' perennial patterns
                                    endless as
waves' plainsong

hope bellied sails
                                    despair bent
backs under clouds drifting like continents
fire cleared
                                    new species grew
slow among the trace elements of dreams and fabulous lies

larks learned summer carols
                                    in years inverted
God and the axe cut back chaos
                                    minds clenched
on flesh trembling meat bleating fearful as moa hunters
cutting their own throats

By decades neat streets
                                    named for Home
echoed trains morose as moreporks
                                    trying to connect
clap-board chapels dairies mossy
                                    memorials
ponga uncurling

                                        no sacrifices
specific generational nor power
                                        can stop the land
going back at the margin
                                        of settlement and
empire
                                        rankness outcrops
love checked becomes the hiss of cold cosmos when the
telly
stops.

                    Point Howard, Wellington

Cuckoo fluted Spring marches
the Renaissance route, thunder drums
each celebrated hump and hollow,
pitting the rainbow Rhine, the rancid Seine,
turbid Thames with acid rain.

Here, untargeted in absurd
September, magpie gangs smart-talk
down dusty roads on bellowing plains,
but Spring is sanity in lands
where butter is preferred to bombs.

Wanganui

In Orcadia, 20th August, 1908

'Between weathers' calm in the world's afternoon:
one smokes and ponders probability; the other
lays down a wash, high Northern blue
over Scapa Flow's imperial depths,
the braided race, the glittering shores of Hoy

his mummy's friend has bought, where they will stay:
Duncan, juiciest of the Bloomsberries,
long of life and limb (Six-five and 93)
has slipped from cousin Lytton, on Brinkie's Brae
sees peat smoke colonnade his huge view

of rounded hills and the far-off southern isles,
Cava and Flotta, then starts again, diluting
from the zenith, his charged brush steady
as it still will be when he is kilted amongst
the Clan Incontinent, an Edwardian relic.

White-maas plane about the shrouded herring fleet.
Bare foot below on Third World wharves salt-sharp
fishwives get to the guts of things and Maynard's
mind bursts into algebraic flower: 'In the long-run,'
he said, 'we are all dead!' and laughed and reached.

Clever bugger, he could browbeat Bertrand;
at Versailles make plain the reason why,
resign at Germany's blinding (As I write,
after seventy years the walls are falling);
an outsider, rich by insider trading,

he saw the hidden hands, how greed replaced
by reason might let the commonwealth begin.
Ah he would marry a Russian ballerina!
Father the World Bank! Arts Council! I.M.F! . . .
but on that far Orcadian afternoon,
loud with the beat of wings, in Duncan's arms he slept.

Wanganui

Suppressing the Welsh

December, 1932, they cracked
the kids' moneybox, came home singing drunk.
Dadda had had two games for Wales, two wives,
two pubs, three kids . . . no means of support when
he landed on my Mum and Dad: twice the mouths
to fill; twenty-odd shirts in Monday's tub.

Down on his cold couch Dadda heard my making:
slump or not, the doctor said, now I was
in her belly, they must get off her back.
Guilt kept her on the attack years after
Dadda had gone feet first back home to Wales.

I saw his dead face in my Dad's who had
'FOOL'! round his neck for speaking Welsh at school
but died talking to Dadda, proud as a bard.

Wanganui

Family Album

Dead son, dead son, I can no longer
hold you in my mind
as once I held you in my arms:
it can't be done, it can't be done.

So I arrange again your smiles,
print dates, chart your curve
beyond our knowing, only here
in God's gravity record the faint pulse
of love's disproof of time and space.

Wanganui

States of Mind

Dizzy with sleep in Double
British Summertime,
bed hot, ruckled as ever—
lasting sunset, I sense pulsing
harvesters shaking the house,

dream of the sunk sun rising
on New York's sky-scrapers, fading
neon lights, peaceful street lamps
dimming as day, like sweet freedom,
is handed across the sea.

'Blinds down! Blinds down, Sir.' Startled
I comply and conceal the child's
geography, blue crayon coast,
purple sky above the polar page,
amazed that unlike the sun,

to go to America
nowadays you land at L.A.
Belief suspended, music
swoons; four cinemas long, seven
miles high, we pursue Dirty

Harry through the Arctic sky.
Above the Law's wet leniency
with his magic gun, he blows
problems away and his fists knock
democracy into shape.

Blinds up, released for plastic
trays, I watch blank pages riffle:
no sign of life, white wastes clean
all dislocated day until
Uranium City where

a light burns baleful bright as
shadows lengthen, turn Prairie mud.
Rockies arch their spine, out of
evening lands coils Columbia's
glistening gut. At Spokane

we sink down towards soft quilts
which shake us; sunlight greys to rain.
Slogans shout BETHLEHEM STEEL!
Strange, terrifying Disneyland.
Our wheels go down into the dusk.

Wanganui

Next Door to Death

Surprising that your dust does not quite fill
the small hole in your lawn. The family

tread turf: widow, children, their kids . . . 'Smile please'!
You enjoyed black jokes, your head adjusted

by carcinogenic drugs . . . Your mother
erected your cross, you said: old Adam

survived, became a Quaker war hero.
Your brother used his head, Oxford don, left

you the tin tedium of a Kiwi town
and domestic disciplines: a good wife,

God. Failed writer proof-reading classifieds
year on mortgaged year, you mowed down summers

bawling hymns, white browed, mad-eyed, one hot night
dying, crying your 'Redeemer Liveth'.

Wanganui

I have heard them
tight-lipped tack
    South
  in a sentence

close-hauled lean
this way and that
trying for headway

whilst reality runs
   deep as History in
their bones and brass
    accents

beneath them
     beyond them
  hegemonic horizons
fall into flat fact.

Day's Bay, Wellington

Flux

Time wears at Skarabrae:
by centuries the sea
frets to bring Skail Bay

under ancient doors, free
ordered stone
from walls to scree

and its mindless monotone
mumbling on the shore,
order overthrown.

Nothing endures;
rocks grind to sand;
spirit deplores

its frailty before the tide's
indifference, self's pride.

Wanganui

Read

Whilst masons amended history
with more heroes dead of the imperial
wound, my aircrew brother, amputee,
was honoured amongst bus queues under
hospital-blue skies that peaceful summer
when oranges came off the ration.

There were white scars on Dad's shins from
the First Contest's poison gas as we sat
on the shore conveyor-belting butties
of sliced bread (mum, dad, three lads)
chucking gulls crusts, rocks at the sea
licking its lips, predator's ridged palate.

The re-opened wrought-iron pier had
muscled legs stuck in crabby pools where
barbed wire bled and on a leeward stall
I found a shocking book in that age
of austerity, pages unused
like morning's ebb shore and words scant as

shells, bright with right simplicity,
or so it seemed to me, blurter of truth
over boarding house starch, brothers'
derision, spilling idealism
like tomato sauce . . .

                It took my hot half-crown.
Here's my fly-leaf flourish;

                   years on, the poet's
neat on the title page . . .

                'O dark eyes,

I am weary of the white wrath of
the sea / Come with me to the vernal woods'
I parodied at parties: over
the top and charged with a yell of self!

But then I learned the pathos of soldiers;
power's bloody-minded nonchalance
and firm clasp of the anarchist dead.

                              As he
was benighted by a war-monger,
so his long hope for an art to salve
like midnight carols or break through in
no-man's land kind as Spring flowers, seems

artless as these poems now in times when
only money can communicate,
art's a commodity, and missiles
fly Orwellian trajectories into
the mumbling future.

                    These live. He's
back beneath the soil his fathers tilled.

Day's Bay, Wellington

22

The Wreck of the Hampshire

Like a medal the moon
   lobs in the folding bay
where Kitchener's sockets
   review ranked star sway.

Gulled streets by culled shires
   he pointed their way, emptied beds
and boots, waged war with shillings:
   profits exploded; the rich charged glasses.

On course to 'inspirit Russia'
   a mine did him the honours.
The East turned red.
   Day has yet to come.

Day's Bay, Wellington

The Solace of Art

There should come a time when life would resolve simple as
Astronauts' Earth . . . but the parent beyond the morning mirror
stares back baffled still. 'Dad . . . ?' I always got the same reply:

'Keep carrying on. Say nowt.' By my age, his muscles gone, thanks
to the market's munificence, he was off on his bike by six and at
his offices, his morning humiliations, the man-of-the-house

'Off the tools, on the dusters and vac.' He was rough on Mum's
expert advice until he pitched face-first in the ditch, heart
broken. 'Ta-ta' he told her. 'Ta-ta, May', but they got him back

grey-faced until he could grasp his pension.
                                        Again and again he
met Spring's offensive with his spade, retreating before Winter
to his hearth; except on Thursdays every blaspheming week for

Evensong from some cathedral up and down the land, basso profundo
in his armchair, echoing those last sounds of Christendom, words
worn away like stone with use, tunes shaped sure and odd as scythes,

day gaudy above the rows of empty pews.
                                    'Christ!' he said, when I
drove him up the Malverns, all Wales at his back, and pointed out
Worcester, Hereford, Gloucester, spires Langland would
                                        have seen,
sharp above the Midlands fug.
                            'Space rockets to search for a sky
god,' I suggested, 'stuck on millennial hold.'

24

He said nothing at
first, squinting across the shires, then softly, 'Talk bloody sense.'

Imperfect Competition

1859–1984

Annus mirabilis!   Mill
honed truth bright as liberty;
Marx
        found mind (save his) Society's
thing;   simian Darwin opposed
bishops with his thumb;

                                        pious
Smiles squeezed blood from the stone
whence Disraeli's angel flew
whilst Marx made revolutions
                                in the grave.

Irony! Perverse echoes
like Crusaders' cauldrons
clanging comfort
                        as reliquaries
to render their bones' beatitude
. . . or Gladstone peering up from
sinecurists' pisspots
for loosing the public school spirit.

Now the competitive paradigm's corrupt:
democratic newspeak shouts voters
to meet the demand of an Elect
(Selected, naturally,
by the Hidden Hand); sense is
taxed from equilibrium; truth's
luxury is a scarce resource.

★

Snow shines on the volcano
but there is summer enough
for cockies to collect;
                    their kids
to rubbish Animal Farm; me,
chalk in hand, to reflect that today
History's polarities
might fuse
          in terminal absurdity.

Waverly, Taranaki

Littoral Love

All day we were stone and water.
Now the salt tangle of love sways
in the lunar tide of your womb.

As we drift deep in sleep together
the singular dead regard
our solace like envious stars.

At dawn I hear the pipe
of migrating birds
above breathing waves.

Life's ritual starts.
I hold you, everywoman,
as I am anyman.

Tahiti, French Polynesia

Bloody Metaphors

Spoiled sacrifices:
   ranked generations grinning
in the dim arcade.

Deadweight dads, tough lads,
   ('Gallipoli'. 'Singapore'.)
part of Empire trade.

Thistle, thrush, lark: Home
   transplanted but **still** elsewhere.
Beyond death? Sepia smiles.

They made a garden
   of Eden: paddocks, Maori squared;
killing chains taut.

Tribute's still paid in
   commonplace atrocities –
lambs jolt by like Jews.

Bloody metaphors!
   'Take, eat,' grunts Te Ruapraha
at Tenderkist Meats.

Above gum-pocked streets
   the moon melts like certainty
in the morning sky.

Wanganui

'Resembling Stupidity'

'We have maintained a silence closely resembling stupidity.' Neil Roberts

Imagine lonely 1 a.m. and
this last will of 'a nice young man'
with a good 'U.E.' and an aerosol can
and a bomb strapped to his chest!

Kilroy's protest against death's whitewash
was more self-regarding, Neil, than what
the Press, with Kiwi ingenuousness, got
right: your 'painstaking' writing on the wall.

They splashed headlines in your ikon blood:
'PUNK ROCKER DEAD' . . . Pavlovian epithets
('tattoed' . . . 'pink-haired') are more powerful threats
still, I'm afraid, than your Bakunian bomb.

New lenses swivel, programs scan within,
read 'bad' for 'sad' and 'mad', unease uncured
('for every security must be further secured')
and most have forgotten your steady hand.

Wanganui

Before detonating a bomb in the foyer of the police
national computer building, Neil Roberts neatly
printed a message in a nearby public lavatory.
This also was seen as little more than vandalism.

Putney Church, 29 October, 1647

Colonel Rainborough to Cromwell
before the representatives of the regiments:
'I think, sir, that the poorest he
that is in England hath but a life
to live as hath the richest he . . . '

A year to the day he was taken
at his word, a Sunday early
he was woken by a sword . . .

Leviathan greed consumed the age,
voided that chiliastic charity,
wiped the soldiers' victory . . .

'Have an eye to property.'
Cromwell's son-in-law required:
they were beaten from parish
to slum to colony. Civil war
is endless when property is king . . .

Except for smart troopers of
Cyril Burt's Horse, bowler-hatted
roundheads who swear, of course,
truth's a daily column-inch between
the thighs of bawds and know
the rubber's mightier than swords.

They cannonade train doors and push
above their station by cash-registers
on ash-heaps,
                    their rewards are mortgages
for life, cars polished off on credit,
due propriety for corgis, Hawks in the Rain,
Grey Rabbit and Pooh, Watership Down –
for all those dumb creatures under the crown . . .

but hush! Animal Liberationists
are padding the town.

Wanganui

Berlin

Four times Troy
the siege lines have lasted
where History stopped in its tracks
and rusted
        twisted barbed, brambling
the high towers locked with curses
where reality sleeps with
no sign of princes or ominous horses.

In youth I defended
the indefensible,
        at 0300 heard my voice
rebound ardent from the Funkturm
with the crackle of Cold War frost
which kept Achilles keen, Hector hot:
the world in slogan simplicity . . .

I was appalled to find their defences
faced out, not in: video ergo sum;
Berlin, Ich bin.

So the materialist frontier holds on
leaf, lake and mind; concepts turn
cul-de-sac   blank.
Passwords   fail.
At the border posts meaning is
smashed
upon the page.

Day's Bay, Wellington

The British Museum

1849–1883

Seasons, years illuminating
capital beneath the rotunda,
carbuncular with prophesy,

describing the spirit's freedom;
shackles of the cash nexus;
determinations of profits:

who would have believed,
patriarch of intellectuals,
you prescribed the mosaic of History?

Bourgeois, Jew: you hated both;
exile, like god and nation, you
left out. From slavery the long march

began through your texts; Lenin entrained;
Mao took the first step; Granma set sail;
Cheka's psychiatrists checked your loyalty.

Meantime you wait on Comrade Fred
to come South with notes for rent
and on the condition of the poor . . .

WAGES ARE A CHARGE AGAINST PROFITS,
EARNED ON MONDAY. THE REST OF THE WEEK
BUYS PALACES, YACHTS AND GUNS,

WHILST IN THE PROMISED LAND (Heads beat assent,
fists phallic with the lyricism of the masses.)
NOBODY IS ANYONE'S COMMODITY. (Even the State's.)

Your children die for want, the silver's sold,
and outside costermongers cuss and yell
like all the tribes of Israel.

Point Howard, Wellington

Socialist Realism

History still waits on its tracks in Europe's station.
Its driving wheels glint, brasses burnished, steam hisses
and the firebox gleams heroic red on the driver and his mate
above the banners, band, bureaucrats.
                              Already late, they
watch the endless speeches, farewells, official kisses;
the grovelling guard's despair and porters' perturbation.

First-class in non-existent: off goes the Station Master's hat!
Second-class has hard seats: there must be errors in the timetable!
The buffet's fit for pigs! Route, destination, can't be true!

Beyond spiked gates buskers profit from the policed, patient queue
of ordinary blokes, their mothers, wives, and kids, whose babel
cannot cohere for confusions, platform complaints.
                              Their diktat
is short and simple: if that mass should move forward half a pace,
barriers would collapse, officials fly. As yet they keep their place.

Day's Bay, Wellington

Ontology

Continuity is our essence against the stars!
from the mammalian rat beneath
saurian contempt in its neural maze
via dark instants of generations
in flickering nights, to filths of profits,
the comradely coughs of viral peers,
we come from particle to noun to
question.

Mapua, Nelson

APPLE
ISLE

Letter from Tasmania

At week-ends I walk an estuary . . .
print my feet on this trail of days,
your absence in my spirit's ebb and flow.

I walk remembering Mahler: Ferrier's voice
rising, surging in my mind, familiar
in its channels and pools as the tide

slaking dry hopes . . .

                    It's safe here.
Legal nets catch fair-sized fish; papers
flap and scream; people concern themselves
with their own reflection. The sun shines

but reality seems a mirage of satellite
opinions, canned laughter, roads running
into melting horizons, pocked

by creatures which have collided with
an incomprehensible future . . .
My colleagues jostle. My students are
amiably unread. Both prefer notes
to books; ignore the life; forgive

my age, almost my enthusiasm.
                        Hurry.
Walk this ephemeral sand by these
empty seas.

Rosevears, Tasmania

Woop-woops

At the red dirt crossroads sheep gasp,
bailed in shade beneath an oak.

Dust rolls. Gums rattle. Steps rise to
nothing but glare. A garden grew,

the corner cropped. Wrought iron wilts,
headstones, sheep-tended, lean all ways.

I turn from this dry narrative
but plastic flowers splash fresh earth:

a new grave, stone proud-polished
as a Sunday car . . . And room for more.

Poatina, Tasmania

Conviction

i.m. the Tolpuddle Martyrs

The inverted moon
mirrors wrongs as right;
as evil, love.

The law's lunacy
is the cracked last laugh
of the jackass!

Hopes fly like bouncing
shadows in the embered
shepherd's night.

Power is knotted:
knout, noose, cat,
regulations like nets . . .

frosted webs the lucky sun
could make tomorrow's
bright jewels!

Ah, what if my hearth
is cold, my children's cries
shaped by soil?

Shall I lie still amongst sheep?

Legana, Tasmania

Print rivers. After-images

From heartbeats on still Australian nights
ships tower the lawn with lights weird
as galaxies, checkpoints, Kantstrasse . . .

After rice grass hisses like static
on airways where jokers spin, rap, speil
zany cartoon worlds all night long.

Sick of homo Geneity, Multiple
Universe Theory, I thumb them out . . .
in silence begin the internal audit

which sank ('In Gold We Trust') Pound;
froze on the Arctic air Mandelstam's
white words for a future Spring; or bore
Auden back to Isis's barge,
grasping his asp, an ancient cottager.

Soon the river will mirror cloud maze,
flight thread . . . but there's no escape
from the beast within, words turn growls,
barks, whines along supermarket alleys.
Once his steel tread in the night streets
standardised minds or made skulls drinking cups
but now, via ratology, lights blart bright offers,
at check-outs conned by C.C.T.V., choc bars
stand priapic by razors; Di and Fergy smirk;
white noise soothes the piping till and blinking,
laden, we are impoverished . . .

Today my classes, raised on prime time
blood will find Lear's gabble, the Fool's,
Poor Tom's, dull as Gloucester's vision loss
or Cordelia's vertical slip, the world
crashing into blank meaninglessness.

And kids with televisual access
to the Presidential rectum have junked
with yankee doodlings 'WORK–CONSUME–DIE'
above commuter tracks and reason
                              breaks . . .

'River run past Eve and Adam's door.'

Legana, Tasmania

Mella Dan

It's gone down now, ice-decked, docked in polar dark,
that vibrant orange ship which budged the Hobart wharf;
flags slapping with cold South's nip; cook and his mate
leaning, watching bearded men bouncing the gangplank

with their bags, waving down but grinning to each other,
exchanging winks, firm hand shakes . . .
                                        And I was envious,
remembering that camaraderie of men in hazard or with a

common task: my platoon swinging down some dusty road;
those sports teams in the past.
                                And so the expedition was
pulled apart by the tender grasp of women, kids staring up

in the chat at the Mella Dan, helicopter secured aft,
whipping antennae, spinning radar scan, half-forgotten
face of the happy man delivered up again to the bank,
career, garden, women's expectations and pent desires.

Hobart, Tasmania

44

Joining the Imperial Bourgeoisie

Bright as their regimental cap badges,
morning sun shines on crop-headed conscripts,
officer-cadets, temporary gents,
oiling their rifle bolts and easing springs.

It is all good chappery: some brown-nose
instructors making up teams . . . 'Flower of
the fucking country!' the RSM screams
back on the square. Oh it is just 'not on'
not to be keen on shooting, hitting the bull.

The wind cracks red flags down the range;
snatches officerly cant; details march:
under the cloudy mystery of Wales,
beyond the bucking company marquee,
estuarial lawns run emerald down,
ravined and mollusced, to the Irish Sea.

Smartly we slip away, employ the fieldcraft
we have been taught, below the rims of streams
build dams, play like kids all day: Max, destined
soon in Penang to charge into his own
covering fire, a farmer's only son;
myself, poet, gagging for thirty years
on thoughts 'not on' before Australia;
both eighteen, enjoying the higher talk
of God and Englit while the brine wind blew and
bullets flew
            then sliding back like spies from
the estuary of the Dee, scruffy as
the keenest shot amongst the rank and file.

Launceston, Tasmania

45

Saying Goodbye to
the Senior English Teacher

i.m. Lewis Bardenhagen

Tomorrow you will be told.
Today I find you sunk
in the hospital bed.

I stir you, ask advice:
Wyatt, Surrey, Sidney?
'Civility in cruel times.'

Mutability we discuss –
but not yours. Outside trees lose
last leaves. Day declines.

'Keep well', you tell me.
I walk out. Someone moans.
Outside the light is red.

Launceston, Tasmania

KARL MARX
1818-1883
DISPLACED
JEW
BETWEEN OLD
TESTAMENT &

NEW   YOUR PEN SCRATCHED A
SPACE   GODLESS RACELESS A
CENTURY TAUGHT THE RICH TO
GRASP CERTAINTY IN ERROR
BREW CONFUSION AS TRUTH....
THEY SAW SCYTHE AND SICKLE
HACK BACK RANK CZARIST DEC
ADENCE ERECT YOU HERO-ICON
OCLAST AS SAINT......POLARITY
SEEMS THE NATURE OF THINGS
THAT MIND'S SLOW DIALECTIC
SIMPLIFIES   IN HOPE. LONDON
HIGHGATE   CEMETERY

Blew Kennedy's mind (CUT
TO CLIP. REPEAT AD NAUSEAM.) in
slow mo . . .
then the cocacolonised
world's as Bobby resurrects,

                                    a dream

in the shower: Ratings slipped
and what Plato envisioned was
nothing but a flicker on the wall.

Meanwhile, back at the family bar
(CUT TO CLIP. 'STAR'S KIN SLAIN.')
it's Bobby's folks who've got
the bullet . . .

That's mediacracy!

Now is the **Prime Time Golden Age**
(The irrational is the real)
when the **World Circus Presents**
(Sponsored by Bethlehem Steel)
Strike One against the **LIBYAN RED SOX**
on   the   box!
That's mediacrity.

Do not adjust your heads,
there's a fault in reality
and even the old actor
can't conceal
the sunset credits rolling the last reel.

          (SLOW DISSOLVE.)

Launceston, Tasmania
48

Video

For Stan Smith

I slow march the vicar and his flock of bleating boys,
freeze him in his pomp between the crammed front pews of
yawning middle-classes bothering Grod in half-moon glasses;
then REVERSE the lot back to the titling shot:
a finger-post to Yeovil pointing where cauliflower cumulus
boils above Summersit, as Ezra might have writ.

('Dada' the thunder says.)

There's a shot of his foxy farceur mask later: not quite
the full quid, his Dadda an assayer, the son a player
of parts, jongleur, jingler, wandering Jew

hater, and like pater, an expert on gold . . . In the age
of mechanical reproduction with a finger, as Valéry supposed,
FASTFORWARDthemback

PAUSE

at the pastor swinging his censor as if it had spikes,
CUT to Frank Kermode confiding Old Possum went there once
'a hot afternoon in '37'. FLIP to a clip of the local hunt's

clop of horsey I-ambs, a chorus of cows' rural idiocy in
buzzing shade, flittering of swifts, boiling cauliflower . . .

WIPE

to Ez. exaggerating Vesuvio's height as he steps ashore
en route from cage to castle. American Rasputin, he had such
a feel for it: courting fame, editing the ideology,
modernising
the modes of literary production. He married a Shakespear,
made Eliot and Joyce, an amateur of even the perennial Hardy.

49

The machine will not dwell. Glinting, crack-brained,
                                        saluting
the dead Duce,
                his hard image
                        fractures.
                                Pastoral will preserve him
in some amber afternoon: an ivy-banked lane loud with church bells
announcing the invasion of TV's umteenth shot at beatification
of urban neurotics . . . DISSOLVE to a cathedral where actors sprawl,
doing the proles in different voices, sermonising like bishops
until I squash out the sound. FADE

                        to some cloister to murder
St. Thomas, actors static as columns of old English sun.

                                        Guy Fustian
had the 78s in Dortmund; as even books were bad form, played
them quietly in his room, face cracking as the knight's tone
slid into cold command. He loved power, breaking sergeants
pleased him; in Berlin laughed sick in hearing how Hess,
hoeing his row in the prison garden at Spandau, took off his
hat and pissed in it. 'Hitler's Number One!' he'd crow.
Yanks, French, us, Muscovites, took turns to guard Hess.
                                        How dare he,
aged 47, fly a Messerschmitt straight through Britain's defence
with an anti-Commie pact?
                        I see his iron crosses swooping,
quartering the kingdom, castle by castle, counting the Heils,
never landing until, decades later, they cut him down in
Spandau's garden shed,
                        fallen silent as Pound.

The actors do their monologues, sententious twats
(poetic word) milking the last cultic drop, vacant as
the gathered choirs from round East Coke in Mummerset,
consorted as the academic pack who magnified his name.

How they dogged his smart-arse footnotes, made doctoral
exegeses of unimpounded fragments from his European
culture feast. He re-ordered their history, James Jesus
Angleton's mate, with his cut-glass accent, medieval mind;

left the literate streets to Hollywood. **His** King Charles' Head
was proof positive the Parliamentary axe cut
                                    heaven adrift
so democratic scrofula must rage untouched.
                              Best to encode
the texts, cloister them cerebral, heartless against
the Dark Age of the Common Man.
                        I hit STOP. CHANNEL CHANGE:
unremarkable atrocities jerk past, sick pleasures of our
self-destruction . . . then balm of ads. needing only libido
and flash-card literacy.
                 That's all elites require just now.

Rosevears, Tasmania

Letter

Dear wife,
          writing at midnight was simpler.
Now life's punctuations, parentheses, syntax,
stiffen this wrinkled hand; bathos
is my shining crown; words will not offset

          our separation.

Today, blinking to watch your flight lift away,
I was afraid that more than stars or waves or time
might intervene. If it could.
                    Yours ever with love.

Hobart, Tasmania

Islands

For Tim Thorne

The Rev. R. S. Thomas on Bardsey

When wind failed to make maelstrom, sink hopes,
drown prayers, saints landed with their bones
amongst the glistening weed: 'Step in the puddles.
Easier drying socks than mend ankles,' boatmen yelled.
Bags, food, kids, went hand-to-hand ashore.

Oxford reading party, anxious for our books,
eyes bright, we polished lenses, looked about
the Celtic chapel tumbling fifteen hundred years,
unready for long-winded lectures which taught
the virtue of the mushroom, blackberry, sea-wood's
blue flame against rain-silvered dawns . . .

In that first week when we believed
our trajectory straight as Zeno's arrow,
we recognised a face, bleak as Christ's
Probation Officer, gritting English greetings,
binoculars on the pitiless beauty of raptors
against the pilgrimage of innocents.

★

George Mackay Brown in Orkney

Against the white sea's shocks a harrier
         hung
              like catty-face death
tilting along the stone dyke by the empty
fair
where gusts tugged roundabouts rocking
horses grit spattered buckled booths
and Perry Como sang – Fly me to the Moon

which rolled amazed at noon in the litter
of cloud
           and down the slabbed street
the huge voice garbled and boomed
                  with gulls'
applause above the Pierhead crowd
               cheers steaming
as drunks scoffed pies on the stage staggered and
spewed so gulls skirmished and swirled.

The poet looked down on the quays
for his silver harvest of words
             across at Orphir
for flexing corn to winnow his myths
Our Lady of the Harvest golden as
             the ale-house muse

the Orkneys tight in his skaldic fist
between flat palms his lunar face finding
nothing remarkable except the soul's swift
flight from dark through light
            into dark.

*

Thorne on Tasmania

Tasmania's not like that: secular;
few hermits in their cells of meaning;
some poets clutching at truth in media blather . . .

and Thorne, intent as a question mark
on what rests upon genocide
and slavery, eyeballing grabbing bastards

still avid for the tiger's bounty, turning
a penny writing captions for the jail-bird's
ornithology, gives away art in the streets.

Launceston

Threnody for Shirl

Over Tamar's flow you saw cloud flight
                              days spin
out of mind
                      cushioned by drugs
bewigged   your violet eyes huge
        I wished that I could tell you
Jesus and his angels were beyond
                    the withering
of your fair flesh   I wish
our unique entities were
                    solace enough
but Earth's the flat certainty
                    yet
nothing is beyond doubt
nothing   that's death's crux.

Rosevears, Tasmania

Taking the Piss

The sun wakes me from thirty years ago:
a drumming tent in the Grünewald at night;
the gormless major, double-barrelled, long
discharged; the CSM who swopped wife and
medals, pension, kids, for the padre's
batman's bum; sundry sergeants full of beer
and jovial servility; myself, callow subaltern,
disgraced by the sodden troops outside our
beery comfort; Colour Sergeant Griff, whose
mad bull eye belied his drollery: This sergeant
had no balls, the other, clap! I was a male whore!

The Major roared. Barking, bellowing, the rest were
half a pace behind.
                    I faced his rank contempt,
then shoved out into the pelting dark past men
stoic as cattle as laughter surged behind me.

Sudden, ropes were slashed. Bellying canvas
burst as expletives. All night I watched the sky
beyond the Russian wire.

                    A flare!
The kookaburra sun has come.

Rosevears, Tasmania

Prodigal

A chauffeur shows my name, salutes!
A prodigal's return to where
I nosed the wartime wire with Bob,
My dog, watched Hampdens broadcast
Parachutes like dandelion seeds . . .

    I should have asked Cammaerts, SOE:
    'Francis, did you ever see a fat-kneed lad?'

This carpark was Raingill land, lost
As Max, commissioned at Chester with me,
Left red blossoming in a Malay tree . . .

    That spire's above Antrobus graves,
    The wilting Grandpa I watered
    With his feeding cup, his last,
    My third summer, our eyes still locked . . .

Above the smog I'd glimpsed Welsh Wales,
Land of our Dad, who could two-clout
Nails long as your cock BAP! BAP!
Whistled at life after Arras;
Turfed our Anderson shelter under the oak
Over which the thrumming Hun flew 'K.L.M.,
Then L.M.S. from Crewe,' Dad said.

And wrapped against the frost I saw
Searchlights knit scarves from stars, like Mum
Who now is blind to them as Hodge.
Our father is in Devon, dust like Bu,
My boy, whose smile blows in the hills . . .

Thailand, Greece . . . in transit I saw everything/
Nothing. Here the air is warm with ghosts.

Next to the driver, Aussie-style,
I find the city we once went to
Has itself arrived: not only youth
but all its scenes are gone under
streets where rubbish rolls, Blacks wait.
Outside the hotel a beggar grasps.

Inside I stick out my hand. The chauffeur
Inspects it
            but steps back. Salutes!

Upstairs the room's designed for thieves
And on the box with landlordly assurance still
The striped-tied Junkers jaw with scornful eyes.

Midnight or Two p.m., it's too late to call Home . . .

Legana, Tasmania

59

Modern Greats, 1968

Some days it was ten fags or the bus.
I stumped up the river above
the Big Lasher like the Scholar Gypsy

facing expiring dreams, cigarette
unsmokable in pelting rain, considering
my feet in the world's mud, the world

in my head. So time passed. Isis dimpled,
swans arched like questions, boating
about the antique barges, waiting

for answers crenellated colleges could afford
to ignore like the opportunity costs of
stock units on their broad pastures

browsing on the best in the thickening air,
content as the collusive centuries.

Legana, Tasmania

Life Class

Sue lies dutiful,
model of patience
and most beautiful.

Neat, baby-tender
shapes belie the strength
of her soft gender.

The simplicity
of her dark groove: where's
holy mystery?

We shape her, stipple,
scratch, draw nothing for
her highlit nipple.

I sit back; remote
in the blizzard sky
dead, cold planets float.

Statutory lust
is beyond me, near
sixty I'm not fussed.

Smut must grow from fear
of things-in-themselves,
not as-they-appear.

The bright eye makes real;
mind masks the silent
dark senses conceal.

'Change? Or stay?' she asks.
Nobody answers.
Charcoal cracks. Sue basks.

ISLAND CONTINENT

‘*Wara*wara’★
★
★

Transactions in the Language of Late Capitalism.
Australia, 1988.
★

Vessels vague as Endeavour balance like
trade on currency; gulls scream brockerage.
★

**‘Through the glasses they showed no sign of interest
in the ship.’**
★

The city’s a block graph of site values
against the Kondratieff curve of hills
★

‘Neither nails nor beads conciliated them.’
★

and the air is full of waves eroding
commonwealth with verisimilitude.
★

‘All they seemed to want was for us to be gone.’
★

Day One, Term One, even after thirty
odd years I am nervous, up too early,
at the margin counting diminishing
returns, far out opportunity costs . . .

Williamstown, Melbourne

n.b. ‘Wara-wara’ apparently meant,
not ‘welcome’, but ‘piss-off!’.

Capital Ship

Above the Black in the bow
discs spin and track cool
green games; digits twitch,
fingers flicker;
Wall Street   waits.

'Is all life in the balance
of a false profit?' asks
the Black in the bow,
rifle cocked, eyes skinned
by Gulf simmer and glare:

speculation . . . unlike
Gaylord missiles, Vegas
weapon-systems, the whole
hitech superstructure
which will require

profitable replacement
if the Black in the bow
malfunctions, gets the point,
or misses the mine, is
liquidated.

Yeah, at the bottom line
mine-sweeping's a drag
(on the market)
says the Black in the bow.

Newport, Melbourne

Twenty Cents' worth
of Humanities from the Western Suburbs

On a hot Altona afternoon
that obverse face appears . . .
vague as Empire; flattery
forty years ago
             now scribbled
from the coins' impress by
Zoran, Silvana, Hai and co.

I recall the converse, images
at imperial frontiers turned
barbaric blobs, tokenism of
free whorls . . .
             Hai only sees
detritus of the white flood
which washed him here, his
sisters away . . .
             The others joke:
'King Zog? The English Queen!'
prefer the coin's reverse . . .
'It's a free country . . . sir!'

It is.
        Legions of young men's blood
washed and washed again at
the original stain: that Empire's
done, its votaries
             out of mind.

Eager
between two worlds
             the platypus
swims   free!

Altona, Melbourne

Late in the XXth Century

'Hey Professor, you English cunt! You bald-headed prick!'

The air burns with rubber and offence:
a bronze car, white pick-up skidding away,
youths I don't know, Year Twelve girl I teach . . .

'Professor'? They are in some American
teen-age dream, slick as a puddled rainbow . . .
And my offence? Expect too much, assume
hope and a literacy they can't have?

Bond's beery airship blunders overhead;
school windows burn again with Friday sun.
Soon we will be jostling down the freeway
out of the stinking air, fast food video glare . . .

but not them. This is where they are at. Cursing.
Waiting for uniforms in the net of streets.

Altona, Melbourne

For Stanley Middleton, novelist, on his Seventieth Birthday

Trees crack the pavement in Sherwood, caught the boy's
imagination, the master's heel, streets
to school stretching sixty years from Ramsay Mac

to Scargill, bells ringing, set texts tuned as
pulpits and the God of Mines and Sidings
gelding the Roll of Honour: scholarship

boys from chapels, from tin tabernacles,
their way made straight to university's
Rubicon.
          He came back, after school wrote,
year by year, sub-texts to God's nonchalance,
the moon at his winter windows, summer
evenings punctuated by neighbours' shears,

his silences replicating about
the English world in humanity and hope.

Williamstown, Melbourne

Good Grief

or
Hegemony in a country churchyard.

Even in England in grief it's hard to act. I knew
the obituary you word-processed was true,

thus contemptible. I will never understand
how that God Squad girl, half your age, got you in hand,

college chaplain, then tugged you bowing through stately
homes and bishops' courts until suddenly and lately

Rolls queued at her funeral, in your old age
she's buried and you are left spotlit on the stage

of her twee kitchen, boiling eggs on yer tod
and phrasing this which never mentions cancer, god

or much that isn't mannered cant, calendar texts,
codswallop about Stratford and The Bard, Thatcheresque

claptrap, and mostly catalogues (first names) the county set.

That's it? You'll preach on, tell 'em like it's not? . . . YOU BET!

Williamstown, Melbourne

The Distress of the Mature Student

'But my son has died,
my wife was raped,'
he said, and cried.

Dismayed I draped
an arm round him,
sensed the gape

of students gone prim
with contempt, turned
his clown's grin

of pain away, burned
with distaste
as he shrugged, squirmed

from me, faced
them, old, disgraced.

Newport, Melbourne

Williamstown Beach

After night's hot rage,
benches and bottles smashed, day
gleams sharp as cut glass.

Earphoned Desert Rats
advance, toe sand; scavengers
grope in bins, flick scraps.

Gulls scream ignorant
as graffiti; spent waves zip
indifferently.

Arnold long ago
knew God useless as the sea.
Shrewd functionary,

up before the servants to gentle the bourgeois,
he died chasing after History's tramcar.

Williamstown, Melbourne

Friday Afternoons

My grandmother would plant only
at new moon. 'Stick 'em in,' my
grandpa would say and laugh

but she wouldn't: she was a
farmer's daughter from Neston
whilst he was only a plumber

and glazier from Wilmslow as
had been his father and his
and his and they sold paint

and wallpaper and glue from
a little parlour shop which
had a high bell on a spring

I looked forward with my ears
to the loud jangle and 'It's
only me, Mum,' from my Mum

on Friday afternoons when
she and I had been by another
red bus to Stockport market

and met her sister, Milly,
so she unpacked her basket
and gossip and I wandered

where the gas works sighed,
ladders hung, and in black tilth
green plants stepped in rows.

Newport, Melbourne

73

Going Back

i.m. Haydn

Late summer: bowls click, Granelli
rings his icecream bell by the school
where I learned 'Death be not proud'
for this commemorative curb.

It's midnight my time; yours stuck at nine
years and years ago. Oh you were
the boy with the straight bat, the kid
whose goals made me cough with joy!

Listen. Last night I was high hope
over the Alice; a dragon across
the orient dark; in Athens saw
dawn cohere above the wine dark sea.

If you are anywhere outside
this '1960–69'
it's here where I bow beneath
a monkey puzzler, wait upon

silence, hear sparrows' pleasure
at their small accomplishments,
find myself walking for the train:
the station's changed, the destination's just the same.

Newport, Melbourne

Unpacking

Scallop, clam, periwinkle . . . shells spill,
strew the garage floor with kids' short-shadowed days.
I gather up Bardsey, San Raphael, St. Ives . . .
then my fingers falter: a cranial shard,
skull thin, homely as an Easter egg.

Outside I feel where memory echoes
and the life subtends, finger grains
of cold Orcadian shore where bone articulates;
recall the sea-cracked Viking cyst,
the tumble of supernal bones beneath the cliff.

Who, at her grave's closing, imagined this
under song-line stars ten thousand miles away?
I search for excuse, for commonality . . .

For seven years we watched the sun's ship
burn down beyond the Brough where Thorfinn's palace
is two stones high; knew island Spring's flowery
effusion; seals croon summer; like her paced silent
Brodgar Ring: gulls' white cries against black sky.

(And where's that image? In our empty heads
beyond the surgeon's grasp like this poem we make,
me at my desk above the sea, words ravelling,
shadows streaming from my pen. Soon coffee
then the teaching day among the careless,
surplus, hectic young. 'What is mind? No matter.
What is matter? Never mind!' Science rests on ghosts.)

Words. Signs. Runes chopped. Rhyme turned Blood Axe's blade-fury.
Thorfinn hacked a rhyming bishopric my Oxford masters
still enjoy, their drawled convictions full of power's
bilabial expletives, making life sentences
of 'property', 'propriety', 'proprietary':
proper respect offered for a thousand years.

No longer tongue-tied, free to give offence,
I hold this bone key to the word-hoard,
heel the hard Australian earth; re-enter.
Say . . .

Newport, Melbourne

Letter to Stanley Middleton

'Only connect'. E. M. Forster.

Your last novel came by the next post
after I wrote to claim it lost:
that's life's accidental way.

'Some coolie's rapt upon a quay',
you'll say. Well, better to believe
a lascar has a lend . . . the sieve
of hope preserves reason.

              Till One
I read, woke sure ethics atone,
can staunch the Great Novelist's wound;
world-to-rights set out. All around
nocturnal scribble was sprayed: 'DEATH
THRASH ZOMBIES RULE' in black, red wreathed
by swastikas . . . Stan, three feet tall
numb chaos drivels down the wall!

Williamstown

Bond

'La sepultada flor, la sumergida . . .
Cómo se preparó bajo la tierra?'

From **Alstromeria**, Pablo Neruda.

The moon cannot turn
from History
                    nor the solace
of poems
            but stars burn with
glittering disdain
at the economics of Chicago
the politics of the dog.

The President's long dead.
The poet he might have been
sings salt threnodies,

voice breaking where
profits leach from the shore
of the beaten land.

Underground the flower knows
that winters end; spring will be
fragrant as certainty.

Williamstown, Melbourne
In 1970 Chile's Communist Party chose Neruda as its
presidential candidate. He stood down in favour of Salvador
Allende who was elected but assassinated in a CIA coup which
made Chile safe for capital. Neruda died twelve days later.
    The poem was written when the Chilean telephone system
was bought by the Australian magnate, Bond, who was later
imprisoned for some dishonesty. It may say something about
equality in Australia too.

Something Celebratory to Say

i.m. Stephen Murray-Smith
1922–88

I

We spoon four plates of soup,
crack toast. At your age
your grandfather was on
the Somme; your Uncle Don
soon to crash in Burma.

I helped to build the Wall
with decadence: bought
up a flower shop in
East Berlin, filled two
taxis for some girl.

(Emrys is back from
watching it fall; Llewelyn's
off to Tokyo.) I fix
you in a flash: 'Our boys at
Melbourne University!'

Beyond the tinted glass
bright crystals fan; in
their shadowless noons
students slow-motion
the grass, clothes elegantly

torn like ragged-trousered
parodyists, they neither
mourn the triumph of the
till nor millions dead making
the world safe for capital.

Berlin, Tokyo, New York hold
world economy at their
fingertips, scroll futures,
rewrite histories, program
menus for base appetites.

II

I stare at a building
like a slice of toast
where I spent two hours
waiting six floors up
the first time I came here,

watching the Dandenongs'
noonday dance in summer,
cursing to have spent
three hundred dollars
to be where Stephen

was not. How hot and harsh
the city seemed under
its carbon haze, the culture
punitive: far below
undergraduates belted

tennis balls: sport, not
barathea, serge, starched
collars, calico, provides
the necessary pain
to assuage original sins.

Stephen harrumphed when he
found me, supposed all knew
where, for Friday lunch,
he'd be: table full of
talk and glasses, cheese and cups.

Port, I accepted, and some
scrutiny. They frisked me
for facts: books? family?
university? One reached
and turned my glasses off

their lense upon the table-
top . . . then they lapsed back
into committee talk nem. con.,
solemn men who seemed not
to confuse weightiness

and gravity, liked jokes
and heresy. (Did Bradman
ride Phar Lap at Gallipoli?)
They knew the smell of blood,
cordite, and fear beyond

the telly screen: their
generation had seen
the declension from soul
to mind and gut via
via church, school, TV,

the latest tyranny
as heaven turned maths
to depth psychology,
appetites standardised:
end of democracy.

III

'He was a bronze bastard,
commando sergeant, when
I first met him,' said one
of the white-curled gasper,
puffing, pipe or not.

The well-fed, well-to-do
soldiered on when tough
diggers died on the Kokoda
and he had kept to the line
of march into middle-age:

party member, peace worker,
teacher, historian, writer,
editor . . . a man-of-letters,
bold, or rich enough, to have
a rare political nobility.

So afternoon drifted from
Hungary (When Communism
bled red, Suez silted.)
to the silk-hatted villain
in CIA's Australia script;

the forces which took
labour from the land
to mass produce itself;
and profits; the fears
which make working classes

work; the eighteen assumptions
which support 'Perfect
Competition', that paradigm
(that malaprop) which crumbles
to monopoly when any fail . . .

We took a walk. I concealed
my Oxford college began
after he was born. He showed
me the Old Arts Theatre, thus
the way to his wake.

I regret that I hardly
met him, there was a rapport
between us but he was a
sergeant, a tough Aussie,
and I hung back in awe.

IV

His mate the spectacle
specialist had arranged
Mozart for dolphins and
five hundred who sat in
secular silence with

Manning Clarke, Evans
the Globe; with Barry
Jones did not know the
final answer; dumb as
editors, scriveners,

eyes full of salt pictures
of his last voyage South.
In Pomerania
it would have been gowned pomp,
academic grunt, and shove

suitless writers from the doors,
should their self-policing fail,
but amongst these, temper
is democratic: Blainey
of the Overflow praises

the rich ex–Communist . . .
This is a commonwealth of
hope, a vision splendid
to make arid futures green,
turn cold water Calvinism,

corporate Catholicism,
into fine wine; learn
the niceties of rice;
balance of yinyang for
the next millennium.

He read, he said, on
sleepless nights, Gibbon's
calm contemplation, but
wrote with a Leveller's
love and hope for the land.

V

The waitress knows Welly.
He goes to pay. Emrys needs
'Imagist Poets'; Mimi
must oversee packing.
I brim with pleasure,

knowing my sons can join
that company. My Dad
would have said a few words.
Only much later do I
think of something to say . . .

Williamstown, Melbourne

Christmas 1988

i.m. Louis Johnson O.B.E.

Daft in my paper crown I call U.K.,
get Kenyon up for cracker jokes from Oz.

We sprawl at the table, kookaburras
carol, there frost nips, Ken says, 'By the way,

Lou Johnson's dead.' NO! (I hand on the 'phone.)
Not true! There is a letter due from you:

your last was vibrant with curses—Thatcher;
flagellant Brits—just like Enzed; a moan

at drab phlegmy Autumn; bright delight in
Hampshire squirrels . . . You hoarded poems against

late parenthood ('Coming and Going'!) for
the children's Summer you would not see: grim

husbandry but sound . . . Talk to the future, Poet,
prodigious in your box, nose to the cold stars!

Newport, Melbourne

Anima

Of her in his heart he dreamed
grizzled head in her moonlight
fingers in the hot night sweat
between her breasts
                              smoothing
the hull of her hips
                              or thumbs
hard on her throat   her eyes
reading him
                    leaves dry rustling
in the dark world
                              like Sunday
newspapers
                                        affairs
between them left undone

no matter that she was dead in
South America saurian-skinned
wrinkled–dugged grandma
                                        coughing
on a morning cigarette in semi
detached Suburbiton
still he was waiting obliquely
by the window hoping she would
pass
        priestess and nautch–girl
red-haired goddess   alley cat
succubus and love stirring his
doting dream
                    and faithful snore

Newport, Melbourne

Being Determined

Dad? Dad! Smiling there amongst my son's books,
moustached, short-back-and-sides, barrel-chested,
bald as me . . . the same age, just the same looks . . .

a photo I'd forgotten . . . Good on you!
My sons are off to university,
not The Royal Welch Fusiliers like you,

then me. You won your stripes in bloody mud;
I returned salutes with a swagger cane . . .
                                        and

your last words to me? 'You don't know what's good!'
– Mugabe's win the morning that I left –
and five months later you were dead.

No grasping determinations so deft
which sent my brothers, then you, to Transvaal,
me to Australia's authentic life.

Williamstown, Melbourne

Highland Real

i.m. Tam Lawrence

Along wheel-rut summer lanes he hung,
schoolboy watching mudguards and brass lamps
bat down dusty grasses and pre-war days,

steadied by his father's hand, sharp Scot
making country calls by Bliss Gate, Aberley,
Wyre Forest, where Highlanders were chopped

after Worcester . . . A barrel of salted herring,
he said his Dad rolled down to the train each term,
a medical student in Aberdeen, that granite town.

After, in the soft South, the spatted G.P.,
he spared the rural poor facetiousness for
fifty years and more, left his widow to smack

the Colonel-publican's face for a Christmas-
charity kiss, whilst Tam, art teacher, cursed
the charm of the nouveau-riche, hypocrisy, apathy,

with un-English fervour as Thatcher waxed ghastly
as the moon in the Severn, his line floating
across brown, god-glints in twilit silence,

hopes always rising, but aware that flux bore
everything away and his son, orange-headed, lost
in London or Spain, could fish only for a job.

Williamstown, Melbourne

Imitations of Art

For S. M-S

In the margin saved from sleep,
staring beyond images,
I reflect against the glass.

Outside light etches crane and ship,
aquatints sea and shore from St. Kilda
to Sandringham, names thrown together
to impress the frivolous land.

Somedays a paparazzi sun
flares above the Dandenongs, over-
exposes the city's megaliths,
flash dances streets where Benjil's
wattle birds splash expletives;

or covertly pans North, standardising
reds, blues, minds; turning the real silly
as a soap bubble, blue and brief as Earth.

Then, clandestine as a cat,
amongst yesterday's truth and
History's trash, twitching
                             its tail
in self-regard, softly unconsidered
                    my poem goes.

Newport, Melbourne

89

Becoming Australian

From a tent of flags Her Majesty stares
Down at where we wait on ceremony.
Babel builds. All kinds of kids slide and yell.

'About bloody time!' a ripe voice informs
His Worship, processing in his chains and ruffs.
He blows in the mike, starts, says four times

He's fifth generation Oz, murders the M.P.'s
Polish name, nods to Polly Glot, his clerk,
Who raps them out, no sweat. We line up, swear
Or affirm loyalty to the photo.

Republican Pom, doubly smug, I say
'First' for 'Second' but feel a right burk:
Vietnamese weeping with joy scotch my smirk.
We get our potted wattles, tea from the tray.

Williamstown, Melbourne

Night Piece

You know
the pillow's yoke
                    of
regret hot grief
opportunities'
                    costs
bits left unsaid
                    which
make you toss
                    me turn
Southern Ocean swells
to steam trains far
off on frosty nights
                    when
even beyond Handforth
                    I
could hear the spondee thump
of strength
                    sense the rhythm of
iambs imprisoned in the rails
and tired poetics of First Class
sleepers
                    sure of
                    bent backs
                            tons
shovelled whilst the driver stares
at certain history grateful for
his job.

      Aaah fifty years down
the line you can still hear
tickety-tock
         the family clock
taking its measure
of you.

Williamstown, Melbourne

On the New Parliament House

Canberra, New Year, 1990

From rock, from awful ochres tempered in sunfire;
from bush burbling idiotic, inane plains; from
seas wordlessly folding and smoothing shores; from
plagues of flies, floods, and pestilence . . . under
the lash of profit's necessity, blood beating Europe's
surplus labour hard as iron in the desert wind; in
seven generations into the clear air, this
is our apex: Earth has nothing to show more fair.
The building demonstrates democracy:
polarity fusing to support the synthetic flag
which continental winds shred and tear . . .
a roof of grass which axe, sheep, ice turned
capital for this millennial moment when
both dogma and decadence crumble and despair.

PENINSULA

How sweetly birds sing on Sunday

How sweetly birds sing on Sunday
when we have made love
and morning sun strokes our paintings,
pots, photographs of the smiling dead.
Our bed's dream-rack is soft, pillows
smooth as we shore up seconds against
time and the cats' impatience upon
the window sill . . . Such assaults on
this simplicity the weekday world makes,
but nothing comes near this loving
stillness, Lady, between you and me.

Flinders, Victoria

An End to Fiction

What was it that I believed in books?

We had a nifty, up-and-over bookcase,
ecclesiastical with stained glass
for the parlour's Sunday best;
                                     one
missing lozenge giving a sight of
Dornford Yates and the diagrammatic
Home Doctor.

Laughing at William and his chums
read by torchlight beneath the blankets
(The girl turned sociologist in later life)
was a mistake, but school cert. 'Kim'
was my cadre at officer selection.

'The Woman Who Rode Away' hardened my
interest: the Northern lad come good in
the aristocratic enemy. (Only later could I
understand how, his flame consumed, she left
his ashes at the station, so keen to get her
new man home.)

                    Lawrence sustained me route-
marching Westphalia, taking a couple of pages
each hour with water along the endless roads,
poplars erect as. . .
honour guards,

                hoping for some fraternisation
with Waltrout, sad countess in her schloss
set among well-dunged fields . . .

                                     'No,' she would say
in her garden, I avoided the gloom of her
antlered walls, 'not like this. Not like the
peasants' and she would prattle precisely,
whilst I fumbled, about her dead panzer
lover of the previous decade.

                                   Furiously
I would bicycle back down the Rhurschnellweg,
air sick with cut flowers heaped on Dortmund's
war dead, nightingales sobbing, grinding my teeth
on her claim that the rest of the world was
right to call the Germans 'a nation of poets.'

                  So I found no such sublimations
of the civil war, all was complexity,
the fury and the mire of baffled balls, books
innocent as the snow in which the Thought Fox
left no tracks, the blizzard of shredded fax
obscuring triumph in the streets;

                                     all channels
showing General Schwarzenegger's potato face and
training films, Wolf Blitzer calling the shots,
von Braun's boys, truth once more a dream
in the total state.

Flinders, Victoria

Entrances and Exits

For Bill Roache on his sixtieth birthday

I

To my Mum Lindow was where
only fast girls would go.

By the black pond's magic their pupils
reflected the sky, moss in their hair.

It was there that the Terriers camped,
came marching at carnival

pre-war, the town's brass bleating,
flags flapping, heart-thumps, boots stamped;

fresh faces clamped, the boys stiff
with sudden heroism and my nape

gone proud as a dog's as folk cheered
above me in the drums' skitter, bang and biff,

me blowing a riff, squeaker unfurled
like a spring, a bee's tongue,

breathless outside Granny's shop,
lost amongst legs in my underworld.

II

Was it that year, doctor's son, you went weeping away
to boarding school, far from Ilkeston's shovelled slag alps?

What a straight bat you learned to play! I just hurled the ball
fast as I could; left at sixteen: white-collar job.

Conscripted, commissioned, 'Orderly Pig', before dawn
I waited, seeing the sleepy sea hardly disturb

Kingston's silent glitter, then your plane came skimming like
a stone over the Caribbean, turned a Merlin roar.

You wore bogus Glen Miller glasses; exchanged salutes;
I was no longer Junior Wart; willy-nilly friends for life

but mistaking Jamaica for the army, signed on,
and away five years of life . . .

III

Then married both, we all
sat on damp carpet
in your actors' digs
at Oldham Rep., a wet
Saturday night, ate
tinned ham and mash, drank

Spanish red. Pubs emptied,
chip shops filled, rain
dripped, the gas fire popped

out: 'That time in Dortmund . . .
on Salisbury Plain . . .
Bermuda . . . ' 'I said

but he said'. 'Bodger-Jones?'
'No, Beasthurst . . .' 'Left-right,
Halt!' A student teacher, I wrote.

You took up centre stage,
stardom, night after night
modelling back-street life,

to and fro in your Rolls,
a pretend prole all your life,
whilst I tried to be bourgeois:

acted, self-policed till
sick of their greedy strife,
delight in beggars.

IV

Okay, 60, you're a millionaire
living by Lindow and the spire where

th'Antrobuses lie in centuries;
you're a keen golfer, Tory, Druid.

Under Alderley Merlin's knights sleep
like stone; the Beltane Prince is unearthed,

skin and bone preserved two thousand years
by peat moss fluid, swart messenger

to the gods in face of Roman force,
crowned with a sword, blood sickled cool, then

choked with a garotte torce, they watched him
go down deep into our history.

V

Bill, it would have made no difference,
forty years ago, to understand
that the only understanding that
is available is acceptance
that there is none: Earth's all accident.

VI

Now flights descend from industrial skies;
shudder the lake in its maze of paths.

Flinders, Victoria

Supernova Anniversary

Forty years ago my mind clenched on you. By
twenty-four life was easy as our morning bed.
We let sweet life into the random world:
'Do owls drink cocoa, Mummy?' The boy ran
into death. His face grew colder than clay
in our hands. At dawn, our bed still warm, we
could only conceive of love, having made him,
make him again, pray he might intercede.

Outside snow bandaged streets. Chill English days
turned Spring. We bought the cradle our grandchildren know.

From the Australian coast we chance to see,
a star explode and scour a galaxy,
before Earth fuse the heavy elements
human lives require . . . that there might be light.

Flinders, Victoria

Memory and the Etching Studio, Goldsmiths', London, during the 'Winter of Discontent'

'They have the power of description and we succumb
to the pictures they construct'
Salman Rushdie *Satanic Verses*

Waiting my turn at the press, stillness prints:
frost bites like acid, London chokes, etches
halftone; white as a tite St. Paul's disdains
corporations' competitive pricks;
                                    Donne,
poetry's priapic martyr, fingerer of soft
purses, swallower, wallower, saint
of the parvenu, twists death-proud in his shroud.

Erasmo, Spanish dynamo, yells flamenco!
. . . .Stamps out anarchist prints, spreads them
scuffed as the frozen college field (The land's
solid for the gravediggers' strike) ignores

with the frigid chestnuts, whose hands cannot applaud,
the orchestra repeating endlessly,
bourgeois-nostalgic Elgar One, last chord.

Somewhere my goateed neighbour wags away
at Locke. 'Cheap day, Hong Kong,' is all I hear him say.
As winter always astounds our railway line
we join the philosophic army marking time,

commute via Hume, Mill, Russell, Wittgenstein
into the smog. Meaning disconnects; we crane
anxious we might have caught the wrong damned train.

In the Life Room the crippled dancer spreads
her negative. Charcoal scratches, rubbers
highlight: daddies' daughters, dress designers,
shape her in white interrogative light.

On her brown bum are whips' white curlicues;
tight-scrotummed I try to look away:
Boksburg, Transvaal's where my brothers stay.

What then happened here? Did these moths, eyes aflame,
fire Herr Schmidt's burning ambition once again?
Did he sense Australia soused in a full moon

heady as Wagner on FM? Europe
to heel, the Rhur's war aims achieved, go back,
no questions asked?

                                I'd no idea of this
conifered cliff house, Bass Strait's senseless song,
drawing the Weald under Boeings and larks
by Shoreham, in the stark boughs magic apples

bright with stored summer, where to celebrate
Palmer's centenary, cement Blake's vision,
down the Darenth Valley to Deptford, loud
and malodorous, the motorway hoons flow.

It seemed the best thing to be up and go.

Here reality is hard edged as shadows.
Endeavour slid incomprehensibly
in ultra-violet clarity past blind

Australians' boats; fancy-dressed
officers saw gums turn elms for decades,
noble parkland stretch; escapees below,

among the export cargo's infinitely
divisible labour force, prepared to
spread siphilisation, in mind-forged manacles

starve in aboriginal plenty.
Now song-lines are sealed, beach heads
established, propitiatory towers
like bar graphs indicate site values as,
via innerspace, the green figures arrive.

New light dazzles, ultra-violet and
interrogative; the sweet sun corrupts.
This land will not imitate our art;

abused, in love with others still,
its reality seems black shadows, waste.

Privileged by imperial peripheries
we switch on mind and air conditioning,
yet see the centres losing hold, love martyred,
crushed and hosed away by tyrants' fear;
smug greed flog the future with a 'use-by' date.

Reason is our essence, the father and
child of democracy, mothered by words.

Love language, nurture its nuances,
the critical craft of its anarchic excess!

Flinders, Victoria

The Objectivity of the Stars

Tired Dean of Year Twelve, towards the end of term
I cannot sleep, synapses soon
jammed with concerns which schoolday might confirm.

I rise, hear the rhythmic beat of the half-moon
rolling on the shore, crickets trill,
and in the sleeping town a cock like a raucous hoon.

Bare feet hot from our bed on the dewed tiles' chill,
I rub gummed eyes, myopic see
stars as snowflakes and night's blizzard frozen still,

not only for my life's hopeless brevity
but for my vainglorious species
which cannot reduce time's reverse alchemy

by 1 and 0, love's binary scale.
Why something, not nothing? The stars turn pale.

Flinders, Victoria

Epitaph

Uprooted from midden, rain, mud;
in sun-cracked concrete, flaking iron;
from seasons to shifts, saints to Tatts,
amongst factories she flowered,
withered . . .
       What forced her fingers to
peel pages, stitch words, iron sense
in alien English until
her eyes could run along lines, skip,
jump to conclusions, before genes
caught up with her? (Whites again fought
Reds in thickening blood.)
        When she
could no longer walk to class, then
her poems flew:
       Walpurgisnacht!
They stole her lost but literate soul.

Flinders, Victoria

On Your Happiness

Autumn Sunday morning
waiting by the monument
where wind has frayed the flowers
and rain has blurred the messages,

I watch the island a
sunshaft is embellishing,
floating in planes of sky
and tilting sea.

I could fix a Golden Mean
horizon, splinter sticks
of charcoal, scratch the bay's
incision down below;

slap on this macrocarpa
where herons are enshrouded,
scumble chiaroscuro and fake
the sea through foliage . . .

but cloud occludes the sunlight
and dims my vision splendid:
I see you on the white sand
down below, holding hands

with grandsons, hair bright
as yours was, who run to
find you treasure. Ah the day,
the quiet bay, are bright
with joy at the sweet endeavours
of each little boy . . .

Flinders, Victoria

At Another End of History

Autumn, the sun's face turning away,
the moon's compulsion slapping steps down
one
                    by
                                        one
as the tide mounts shores about the bay,
cresting them with cans, bones, plastic wrack.

From the wooden pier lines curve for squid,
sunlight warming fingers at the rail:
Mitteleuropean, Asian, Skip, intent
beyond surface glint; wife, husband, kid.

Clouds tow vainglorious rainbows nowhere;
baulks heave green again, nails proud,
bolts countersunk in another age
of iron and rust, twisting like sleepers

at some scalloped halt where now
no foot alights   empty
as Ostia's wharves when centuries
turned the tide to grass . . .

Do we float? Does the structure sway?
One step now is all it takes for words
like fish to flash away into the dark
ages of the sea, dumb centuries
rolling in remorseless as the scum
at the carpark's crumbling edge.

Flinders, Victoria

**a huge moon
malignant squats
on dark islands her
alchemy gilds**

leaden waves beneath
generations stood
serene mother face
you know she's all
littered like any
the spell snaps

the bluff silence where a thousand
golden as she bends over us
full of love-light swelling but
pock-marked by gum tyre-treads
street of our cul-de-sac times
soon she dwindles lost balloon

Flinders, Victoria

A Day on the Bay

For Emrys, my son

Millions of dollars jingle and nod neglected
flash and chassis by the catwalk white
and wonderfully smooth as cigarette ads
a few in the right gear pose overweight we

slide onto the ferry's blue vinyl fifty
at twenty bucks a bum the bird club
binoculared bright-eyed bush hats badged

put the ferry master in his element winding
his wheel memories the channel of khaki sea
mike buzzing busy as the Wizard of Oz
booming on the balmy Sunday bay

                              'Godwits!'
we tilt above drowned valleys where
Australians walked antediluvian hills
turned islands on the song-lines South
on this brief day of Sun-Moon-Earth's
molten dispute

                   'That's Freeman Point
Penal Settlement.' We laugh but morose
fishermen in rocking boats won't wave
chin-down pelicans disapprove old Ted
wades the aisle egg-head red Daphne alights

retells how once she rode sidecar in the
Monte Carlo Rally tosses curls long gone
the bold bright girl still in her eye

'Gerros!' you said as we parked and will
not see her beyond the avian neck
beaky preening at what's past

your head is full of Paris green politics
and the next essay's need I talk softly
of Cubism's blueprint blown away futures

drowned in the bloody Marne as the imperial
bourgeoisie dared to disturb the universe
sent in the Yanks in bankers' bowlers to
recast the balance souvenir good quotes . . .

You brought me bits of the Berlin Wall that
huge investment paying out at last in gold
for the Axis tin kudos for the West

elsewhere hope but I best recall the road
by the lake at Kladow running into brambles
and barbed wire so absurd even a bird

ignored it but at night in winter
the Russian tanks coughed in summer
on Sunday mornings like this I sat on

the terrace of the officers' mess amongst
white birch trunks like you
elegant with youth
                                   slept.

By the wheelhouse I watch Eliotian echoes
green from ragged claws in the chambers of the sea
black stumps of wharves where life
was measured out with axemen's strokes
(three tons of wattle dried a chickory ton) . . .
                                   'Muttonbirds!'
(Breed late into the night and travel North
in Winter) misnomered wave-skimmers solitaries far
out on the ocean's face under the stars
easy meat
on land as Abo sheilas groped out and near destroyed
but preserving self-conceptions beyond our grasp . . .

                'Sometimes sea eagles . . .'
see our flash of alien concern as they teeter
in insidious intent . . . 'At Rhyll the French kept their
powder dry . . . ' practising pronunciation on cold
mornings before their final cultural cringe

('Hear the curlews crying each to each!')
when the land was peopled by the contumacious poor
and men in rolled white flannels walked the beach.

Evening spreads smooth-browed and broad you are
at the prow I go back where gulls wheels and deal
wake-watching constructing the past I grow old.

Flinders, Victoria

Table Manners

Ibu Oka's face
was closed to Western babel,
chatelaine in place

at flame-lit table
swayed with girls singing gods' birth:
a sanscrit fable.

'Berger means the earth
is left behind by the world:
art has lost its worth.'

Ocean waves furled
white on the Balinese shore;
twilight was star-pearled.

'Well I'm sorry if you think I'm a bore!'
'Okay, take it easy. Tell us more.'

Flinders, Victoria

A Puritan Collage
at the end of the Second Millennium

The library windows save us from Jesus
rock blasting the yard; the kids won't dance,
know everything at school's a con.
                                    The band's
smart van, crucifixion in gilt,
is in good view of where they strut,
magnifying God's name in vain; junk
food's the consuming interest . . . except
to Shane, who needs the confirmation of pain,
provokes: skull knuckled, goes down,
booted, gets up, choreographs
a TV ninja kick: love's dumb martyr,
red-eared centre of attention yet again,
goes sprawling snot-nosed in the rock thump
while we rap upon the pane.

'It's like something on TV.'
'Better stop it all the same.'
No one moves: sickness in our silence.
Music bangs. 'I'd like to give him some.'
'Yeah, the scumbag, he's to blame.'

*

Catechism

'What is your name?' The book was worn,
the answer, 'n or m' a holy mystery when
all we had were our shy syllables whispered.

Ma Sellars' glasses sparked, her ruler stabbed:
'Who gave you this name?' Now we could chorus,
'Mygodfathersandgodmothersatmybaptism

whereinIwasmadeachildofgoda . . . ' Slyly we watched
Anthony tethered by fear at the playground's centre
and the maypole hatch where **HE** could see him,

hoping for cloven fire to prove OUR innocence
in a flash! His radiant soul was spotted dim
as an electric bulb with sin, we knew:

at Church Road (C of E) Primary, God,
the ruler, made straight and narrow life, governed
with guilt, less flexible than the hangman's rope.

★

Prayer

The fruit is fallen from the tree,
in winter's cave the spirit sleeps.
Jesus, gardener, can our loved dead
truly be among flower fields of stars
beyond graves' black hole vacancy?

★

Pantum

In Christ's second millennium He disappeared
    within two generations of this last century.
Had the kings and cousin-emperors engineered
    machine-gun culls, pre-emptive butchery?

Skewing of sense, positivists claimed,
    was God's gravity bending the light of reason.
To demonstrate Earth as a blue bubble framed
    in black (no sign of borders) is a kind of treason.

Graven images: the President's brains in slow-motion;
   magic mushrooms of the bomb; the Arab mother's oath.
Air and water are no good: scarcity's our best notion,
   our last market contradiction's when they are both.

Force, fraud, white star, red, do for the hermit in the head;
   revolutions of the heart die with the first official kiss.
Soon, Yeats said, we'll make contact with the dead:
   screens will hiss, saints will tremble in their bliss.

Dromana, Victoria

Driving to Work

In Autumn first thing the sun
hurts your eye on the bay road

ochre islands buckle on
the splintering sea April

paddocks undrenched ditches crazed
glint with glass dust rolls stones fly

I say our situation
would have pleased us years four kids

half-a-world away
                        agents
flag auctions acres charted

'work-consume-die' dryly wait
at the limit your hands deft

on freeway's helter-skelter
gold ring bright about the bone.

Flinders, Victoria

Images of Peace and War

Forty degrees. My English class
   Surrenders, listless waits, heads down.
   Mum, then Dad, tip-tapped the plank;
My small son followed, I came last.

Australia's furious, fiery blast
   has burst from its heathen heart.
   In green tunnels sunlight flashed,
The horse clip-clopped, reeds bowed as we passed.

Home, naked, I gulp; see pears
   Smart bombing the parched birdbath.
   Oarless, ageless, we floated
Devon day and dragonfly airs.

Memory shadows lea and leaf.
Cockatoos shriek in Muslim grief.

Flinders, Victoria

New Stone Age

The ditch at Brodgar Ring took
a hundred thousand hours to chip,
Professor Renfrew said. Most of
the skin-clad dwarves did not live
long enough to get a Ph,D.

It makes no sense that in islands
where winter's a nightmare shriek,
short summer the sun's flower kingdom,
they spent life heaving carious slabs
to anchor brevity in steadfast stars.

Absurd as believing that their bones,
deep in Maeshowe's earthen womb,
in receiving the dying sun's last
bloody thrust, made years turn,
in dark caves messiah flowers stir,

grain begin to grow like children,
from the fiery feast, sparks flying
ephemeral into the black waves.

Here, a century or so ago, the land
staked out, codenamed, 'Port Philip Bay'
was full of pacific sky. The Bunurong,
beach bums for forty thousand years,
sang the sun, danced lunar mysteries,

kept to ritual tracks which led, via
pox, lash, bullet, double-entry book-
keeping, to a commodified world bought
cheap, sold dear, or infinitely trashed.

Now the surplus young nod to their music
on the shore; the air begins to burn;
towers which point nowhere, turn carious.

Dromana, Victoria

Avatar

To flies in the cliff's calm
I give the Australian Salute
testily after night's sweat
desert wind's scratch bang

about the iron roof dream-
startled in dressing-gown
at the rail staring down on
flat-stick wind's work on waves

recalling a dawning long ago
when you had cried in your teeth
all night but grasped and cooed
at an orange sun rolling clemmed

in Midland mists raw as Thatcher's
smile that substitute Napoleon
sachet distillation of fete-booming
matrons arrogant queue-jumpers

lying in her pre-Health Service teeth
at some church door for the camera
and the greater glory of Prods
sky thick with filth where we

gave up your little ghost to the
garden of remembrance   abrupt
the burning star flashes over the
island forty degrees promised

I open myself to its hope
head full of green images.

Flinders, Victoria
123

Common Clay

That European winter survivors
turned out of bars like the guard

saw the moon a flare hanging over
loud talk echoing only briefly in

the streets camaraderie made monumental
Dad recalled a lark all beer and no

Boche a secret survey like a recce in
the frost left-right printing out

tight crescents drives avenues of homes
for heroes the man with the book and

pencil gave him a job so our house
came cheaper clay cow pastures turned

trim with privet tulips ranked trilbies
trooping off house names a laugh

on disciplinary mortgage deeds kids
only getting a whiff of something when

winter turned footings mud the trap by
the bright hearth was lifted and Dad went

down into the stinking dark later his
wild Welsh waking us quaking us years after.

Flinders, Victoria

The Lucubration

Rain drums on our iron roof, beats
retreat down the dark coast, night
like black ash presses us prone
as relics from death's dreamworld,
rasping dry lyrics from life . . .
A third alseep! Ten years in
our marriage-bed's bas-relief,

limbs flying in a fresco of
mock youth, grey hair awry . . . You tense
in that paleolithic world
which made us (Lives unchanging
as birdsong through myriad
seasons of the boundless self.)
waiting amongst the sleeping

tribe by the Horn Gates for truth's
crazy dance: prophesies of
plague! Clues to the calculus!
Futures in babies' organs!
Drought in Egypt! A round Earth!
Asclepius, god of the sick,
do we still owe Socrates'

cock? His daemon, not reason's
constraint, let him swallow
Philosophy's accolade
and haunts our footnotes to him
unacknowledged still – save for
sceptics' immoderation,
claims that the rational is real

estate . . . The house creaks. Sea winds
stoop on the Peninsula . . .
Dissatisfied man under
smug stars, grandfather, I fear
for love's trusting innocence
in futures media-bland where
all the world's a stage; actors

are titular talking heads
of state; politics porcine;
wars prime-timed, edited, glossed;
transnationals' interest
screened by cartoon, sport, news with
shots of non-consumers' deaths . . . and
consciousness's intermittent . . .

we are becoming a myth.

The Angel of the Lord lights
in the garden to reveal
the pattern in the curtains,
explain the morphology
of chance: the moon fits the sun,
eclipsing as she climbs, coy
maiden to her marriage-bed,
mind dark with coincidence.

Flinders, Victoria

Last Word

Mum, the sadness is my brittle grief
turning so quickly to concern
that when news comes of **my** dying
my children will give only brief
thought to my love: order a wreath,
figure the will, phrase an obit . . .
all the rest of it.
           And you, if you
could read this, would not pause:
even at the last you were on about
cheap meat: 'Twopence a pound in
Water Lane', you repeat, ninety years
from Wilmslow in Johannesburg where I
never came, ideas being thicker than blood,
and mine in that land, indiscreet
as my voice blurting right round the world
and back
        to ruin your replies,
                  the line
between us falling dead.

Flinders, Victoria

All Aboard

Continually the heads turn, noon long gone,
glancing out past Snake Island to Wilson's Prom.,

domes capped by UFOs of lenticular cloud:
'That's the direction,' points someone in the crowd.

I focus my binoculars on the far
straggle of old mulga scrub, lean on the car,

my world contracted to a Pacific gull.
'Oh, wow!' they say. I tilt, see the sliding hull

hurl through: 'Seacat'! An oxymoronic name.
(Language fails in our cocacolonial endgame.)

It fills my eyes, surging round the island's tip,
seething white wake humped across the tidal rip.

Of no leaf, bird, golden section was it born.
What shaped such curvilinear certainty of form?

I watch it settle, hear its thunder booming
inland as it turns, stare up at its looming

power, three storeys above the sheds its roar
turns crescendo. Cuts. Silence. It glides. In awe

we sense it comes from an abstract world, remote
in silicon lies the homeport of this boat;

in that certain universe solutions flow:
two halves always make a whole, whether or no.

A waning moon is towing the tide across
the low shore, glossing footsteps: there's a pathos

in the silence, the people standing overawed,
grasping tickets, children, bags, eager to board.

Then they laugh: men spin lines, Quasimodo-high,
stare down as if they've landed from the sky.

Like a fart at a party, until too late,
all ignored Cook's 'Endeavour': a human trait.

Cars drive away. It's an ill-wind, they say.
Port Welshpool's a distance from Botany Bay.

Port Welshpool, Victoria

Balinese Ceremony at the Dark-of-the-Moon

Pointed faces make the baby bawl; alien twitterings
don't help. The wife's round–eyed, her mum slit-lipped,
fussing the offerings, her temple sash, a soccer scarf
from Singapore, (ROOSTERS in red) clamps our glib jaws.

He's proud of us, sits us where the weary priest flicks
holy water with white frangipani, shakes his bell against
chatter, drones mantras like a bee in piled fruit and flowers

whilst man, wife, and his mother-in-law step, gesture hope
at each garden shrine, five Big Bens carved, saffron-skirted,
where time's opposite is hollowed against the sun.

Crickets and dragonflies were their diet:
now they have surplus for gods and our disquiet.

Out on the paddy massed ducks flock to their flags,
palms rattle, a black hawk turns on a vortex of prayers.
Bells, flowers and worn stone are familiar as no response.

Saturday declines beneath Agung where we found genuine
smiling squalor; mad-eyed, pole-hung pigs; stink of
chicken shit . . . felt at the roots of Bali where in the coup,

as if on cue, in a purification at the mother temple,
the mountain blew! Red blood hissed like lava in the earth:
five hundred thousand got the chop as these smilers ran amok.

Crickets and dragonflies were their diet:
now there's surplus for their gods and our disquiet.

Under the crater untouched the temple stood while
villages turned ash, bullets flew. Muslim Generals
got down to business with the CIA so big jets boom

over Kuta Beach with tourists enjoying Roman peace,
beer, brown bodies, but whilst crickets and dragonflies
were once the diet, now their population is our disquiet.

He drives us helter-skelter to Denpasar in a chaos of
tolerance and chance. We shake hands. Relax in Departures
chilling happiness amongst beer-bellies, tatts, radiation

burns. The musak thuds, the smoke and gasses rise, and we
are avid to board, eat, drink, watch movies, packed secure
as eggs, slicing the vacuum of the moonless skies.

Flinders, Victoria

Morning

i.m. May Antrobus 1901–1991

For almost a month you have lain
between us in the dark
                I've been
a boy against your back again or
searchlights testing black-out
sirens guns bombs fading
              in your bear-hug
under cover in our snow-cave bed
                fifty years of
nights on
        I wake to your absence
make tea watch day break blank

no trace of you in all this endless
brevity
        against kookaburras' mirth
I write to put you back
        in the rolling world
you made me.

Flinders, Victoria

Without Barbarians

*'And now, what will become of us without barbarians?
They were a kind of solution.'*
C. P. Cavafy

The succubus moon slides
cocks ejaculate prematurely
stars wink at the lyric
freedom of mass dreaming

and the planet's surface pits
minutely under electronic
impacts from incessant satellites
tenderising brains with

dogs' ideals of liberty
maintenance of order so
men love their fists women
caress lovers powerful as

new cars graspable gearsticks
full of revs glossy with
glamour romanticism
is believing there is some

corner of a private pysche
that is forever impenetrable by
market forces daylight
birds singing plangent as

poets in wartime.

Flinders, Victoria

133

Chthonic Dream

The roads were closed, the troops,
pink-faced boys, called curfew cheerfully
with steamy breath. We got across the hills

to mother's: village deserted, her house
full, kitchen stiff with neighbourly smiles,
comfortable chat, a fire ablaze

in the polished range.
                    Don was there,
big brother, broad shouldered, half-
asleep, stretched in an armchair,

his dead mongol son sitting by his feet,
and did not hear his name. Suddenly
the pipes began a gibber and squeak

as the water came back on. We went to
make drinks, set the tray. Beyond the hedge
soldiers waved, bulldozers dug.

Flinders, Victoria

Night on a Bear Market

Dushka, you speak my language,
the lingua franca, d'accord?
A New World Order, nicht wahr?

Okay, while you do that, I'll
talk. The Cold War's over, credit's
unfrozen; but liquidity's

a problem. The solution?
Like the good book says,
'Everything has its season

and price': that's Democracy,
and when I say 'Democracy'
I mean business: cheques

and balances. Vote in the 'Outs',
vote out the 'Ins'? Get screwed!
That's freedom, free enterprise.

It's human nature! Up and down,
boom and slump. Wow, you Russians
sure like caviare! Okay, so you

rent me an orifice but, Dushka,
I'm in the market for babies, right?
Top dollar for good Caucasian stock.

And I need agents with access for
the New World Bankers' Order, Ja?
Da? Oui? Si? Right? Jolly good.

Flinders, Victoria

Being and Time

(Heil Heidegger!)

By the sea epochs
of wrought shells crunch under dumb
chance and our bare feet.

Lungs, larynx, lips make
us and the world: brief gossip
of humanity.

Ibis and heron
whirl up, go back to where waves
gloss, erase our tracks.

Ideas build, drift in
history like shadows or
rainbow miracles.

We are the planet's objects and subjects,
bewildered in our accretion of bones.

Flinders, Victoria

Heart Attack

The hospital on the hill sails into
the night and storm, bells tone, white uniforms
smartly at their stations, the ruthless wind
swaying our curtained privacies so each
wide-eyed man lies in morphine hope, body
anchored by wires and feeds, heart's truth scribbling,
scribbling life's impositions above his head,
knowing now dying is easy as
finding yourself, willynilly, deep
in your darling, the only surprise,
the ordinariness.   The dark is fragrant
with flowers' earthy hope; cards from women
and kids hold us yet we wait like troops to go
ashore where days break like surf over the roofs.

Flinders, Victoria

Child Care in Late Capitalism

Beyond my office door Cher asks,
'Where's fucking Deb and them?'
Bent at my marking I hear the laughs.

Sun shafts the books they never nick:
'boring' now even anguish entertains,
cameras always grab some fly-eyed kid's
pull at a dry pap.

              No sense of sin –
or work . . . bar-coded check-out chicks;
forecourt grunts . . . until robotics or
eighteen, when adult rates send them
surplus down the beach,
                        squinting at
some water-walking skeg, forever
crucified against the sun . . . and when
that's done, fucking Deb and them
grow fat watching soaps ('unreal!')
collecting kids and hopeless dads.

Driving to school I see police lines
prod where for weeks a child's headless
corpse lay in the littered ditch . . .

                      if only
we could find where in the grounds magic
mushrooms loll like Silicon Valley implants,
fat with false consciousness.

Flinders, Victoria

Clear as Day

In the night something has placated the sea
so that pre-dawn dark is free of its bass roar

and I wake quite sure that if, and only if,
the present King of France is bald, I know thee

thus, in the antique . . . If, and only if, I
am the first person singular . . . So I rise,

recall Christ served wafer-thin in cold churches,
foretaste of pie-in-the-sky-when-you-die:

absurd. In my dressing gown and thongs I plod
to the stove, prod embers, load red gum, and feel

anger at archimandrites, bishops, rabbis
in mad hats, predicating this and that of

At my desk I hear, ten miles across the bay,
a huge voice explain why daylight has not come;

may never come again. I shiver, take up
my pen, wait for whatever else it has to say.

Flinders, Victoria

40, a philosopher,
he watched river rainbows slide,
his tower flex museum
windows; then he'd spin, put down
students with Oxford's certainty . . .
until some fat-gut at Kent State
made truth as contingent for good
and all

        incorrigibly.

He rehearsed his farewell speech.
His colleagues gulped coffee and
distractedly, gave him a
bone-handled, letter-opener.

                He
took off for Ultima Thule.

            ★

The kids came home bruised from school,
turned incomprehensible;
light lasted all summer night;
megaliths fingered stars; seals
crooned . . .

        Light left: hurricanoes
flashed, lashed the treeless island.
He wrote spies' confirmation
someone, somewhere had access;
some decent chaps were in the know.

Peats roared in the chimney's throat.
His wife's dog was poisoned. He
sent typescripts south by bottle.

The black kye were killed, buried
in the clover on edict
from Brussels. Milk came tasting
of disinfectant; Tam and
his dad smoked dazed in the byre.
Her ducks were shot. The voice of
the Thatcher was heard in the land.

★

50, at the World's edge, in
Quaker Meeting he studied
Ruapehu's indifference:

the earth moved; the meeting sighed;
the sun circled the Northern
sky above bright Erewhon.

Painter of that sheep-drifted
provisional landscape, he
could neither decode McCahon's
hellfire texts on shit-brown hills
nor the faked relevance of
metropolitan New York:

pigment splattered, pissed and daubed
like H Block cells in Belfast,
but at week-ends, arms linked with

lawyers, teachers, Red riff-raff,
they eyeballed Maori police,
truncheons dented, knuckles taped,

chanted for peace, voices and
banners snatched by gusts among
business blocks, the Texas

with its goodwill cargo of
a million deaths riding out
another storm of heresy.

★

And 60, tattered teacher
in Oz, kids gone, he took to
poems amongst air-heads for whom
truth was the next wave, backs to
the enigmatic continent,

brains softened by cheap TV,
stuffed by sick images,
fast foods, UV, believing
Gulf Oil's war might spill and spoil

their electronic lives like
Hollywood's subtext certainty.

Meanwhile, back in the museum
beneath the philosophers'
tower by the toxic stream,
in municipal silence,

shelved, some mad phrenologist's
Pol Pot bequest, containers
of dreaming, flayed by print, bear
witness to imperial truths.

Flinders, Victoria

Dear Kate, kind daughter

I remember mad joy, seeing the sulphur lights
bloom one by one on his hearse, that he was
coming back to us again, our little boy . . .

In snow-flake silence of the December dawn
in the empty chapel we reached out to him,
but seemed only to push him down:
                              deus ex machina
hummed assent; flame annealed him, made a memorial:
a curb like that which killed him . . .
                              He has been
alone so long, so far away: his Autumn our Spring,
his cold night our warm day, but the bulbs you planted
bloom, you say, and year upon year daffodils and crocus
will bring their solace from that artless earth.

Flinders, Victoria

Ganeesh at Night

All moon-splashed night wind chimes charm Ganeesh
the elephant-headed, moss-blind and far from home
in roses' alien incense, thudding fruit sacrificed
by Great Southern Ocean winds, dark Hindu spirit,
gnomic and silent in the garden
                                    where the naked man
pisses by a lemon tree, aware of the shadowed god,
the crooning lust of mosquitoes, but head back makes
a crucifix of stars centuries of light apart . . .

thinking that if the god should speak, stone eyes
would see a different world; that if huge ears
could hear, he could never explain how folk make
hope from the flux of accidents and coincidence;
prefer diverting impossibility to cold certainty;
persevere in the flesh through love . . .

                                    Memoryless
the moon gapes with perpetual surprise as it swims
round the night. Rubbing spit on bites the man creeps
back to his wife's warmth. Soon beyond their curtains
plovers will shrill enthusiasm, wattlebirds banter,
blackbirds exclaim indignant amongst the fallen fruit
and, under the fiery trees, Maud, 83, chop kindling.

'What kind of a day is it? What's the time?'

Flinders, Victoria

144

Washing Up

In green garden's shade
wind pushes my grandsons' swings:
they are far away.

Dad's garden bolted:
lawns uncut, flowers fallen.
He died in dismay.

Secretly I watched
my Grandpa dying, lying
in sun slants alone.

Before him? Nameless
shadows flying like seasons
on tumbled Welsh stone.

Love does not stem the ruthless chance of things
nor chill indifference check the Winters' Springs.

Flinders, Victoria